Ancients *of* Assisi I

A TRAVEL PHOTO ART BOOK

LAINE CUNNINGHAM

SUN DOGS CREATIONS

Ancients of Assisi I
A Travel Photo Art Book

Published by Sun Dogs Creations
Changing the World One Book at a Time
ISBN: 9781946732453

Softcover Edition

Cover Design by Angel Leya

Introduction

For centuries, Assisi, Italy has been the focus of spiritual activity. Saint Clare founded the Poor Sisters, also called the Poor Clares, in this small Umbrian village. Saint Gabriel of Our Lady of Sorrows was also born there. The ancient city might be best known as the birthplace of Saint Francis.

The tangled, steep streets offer much more than a pilgrimage. Situated in the Province of Perugia, the compact city perches on the western side of Monte Subasio. This part of the Apennine Mountains has been declared a national park.

Inside its borders, people live in tiny villages composed of only a few homes clustered together. They along with their neighbors still live much the way people did centuries ago. This collection explores all these areas and more.

The forty color photos in this book take you into the secret Assisi, the Roman city hidden below the buildings. The ancient Temple of Minerva, now housing Santa Maria sopra Minerva, is one of the few Roman sites that are visible above ground. It is found in the Piazza del Comune, which in Roman times served as a Forum.

The photographs in *Ancients of Assisi I* and *Ancients of Assisi II* were taken at the Basilica di San Francesco, including the Basilica inferior and the Basilica superior; the Sacro Convento, a Franciscan friary; the Rocca Maggiore, a castle that is 800 years old; Santa Maria Maggiore; the Basilica of Santa Chiara, or Saint Clare; and the Roman Domus of Propertius and the Domus of Lararium, both of which are underground.

Of special note in this first collection is a dove that settled inside the Basilica of Santa Maria degli Angeli, recalling the legend of Saint Francis preaching to the birds.

WELCOME

ANCIENT QUARTERS

DEPOSITION

OLIVE GROVE

DEBRIS

GARDEN GATE

AN EVENING WITH MINERVA

ANCIENT AND MODERN

STALAGMITES

SPARKLER

ADMITTANCE

AL FRESCO

TEATIME

ARRIVAL

SERIOUSLY?

ARROW GRAPH

AFTERNOON LIGHT

FORTUNE FROG

GOLDEN EVENING

INVERSION

SEPIA THUNDER

RECYCLE

SCATTERED HEARTS

OBSCURATION

KEEP YOU WELL, FAIR LADY

ESCARPMENT

TOURIST ATTRACTION

FROM THE RAMPART

COMMUNION

INCANDESCENCE

HITHER AND YON

TRIWAY

TRACES

PEACE DOVE

SACRIFICE

VILLAGE ROAD

NATIVE

GUARDING THE GUARDIAN

OVERLOOK

PINK WASH

About the Author

Laine Cunningham is an award-winning novelist. Her career as an artist takes her around the world for extended stays that support research and writing. She enjoys sharing these special times with readers through the Travel Photo Art series.

Novels by Laine Cunningham

The Family Made of Dust
Beloved
Reparation

Other Books by Laine Cunningham

Woman Alone
A Six-Month Journey Through the Australian Outback

The *Woman Alone* Companion Series
On the Wallaby Track
18,000 Miles
Fairy Bread and Bush Tucker
Amazing Australia

Seven Sisters
Spiritual Messages from Aboriginal Australia

Writing While Female or Black or Gay
Diverse Voices in Publishing

CPSIA information can be obtained
at www.ICGtesting.com
Printed in the USA
LVHW081528260719
625481LV00006B/20/P

9 781946 732453